A BOOK OF POETRY

Joseph Jones

Gotham Books
30 N Gould St.
Ste. 20820, Sheridan, WY 82801
https://gothambooksinc.com/
Phone: 1 (307) 464-7800

© 2022 Joseph Jones. All rights reserved. No part of this book may be reproduced, stored in a retrieval system, or transmitted by any means without the written permission of the author.

Published by Gotham Books (August 26, 2022)

ISBN: 979-8-88775-157-3 H
ISBN: 979-8-88775-155-9 P
ISBN: 979-8-88775-156-6 E

Any people depicted in stock imagery provided by iStock are models, and such images are being used for illustrative purposes only.

Certain stock imagery © iStock.

Because of the dynamic nature of the Internet, any web addresses, or links contained in this book may have changed since publication and may no longer be valid. The views expressed in this work are solely those of the author and do not necessarily reflect the views of the publisher, and the publisher hereby disclaims any responsibility for them.

Dedication

I grew up never knowing my true birth father.
Did it affect me? Yes, it did.
But in a very good way. I myself never felt or held then or not even to this day any cold thoughts or displeasure for the man who along with my mother made it possible for my being.

If this person would come up to me today and state and prove that fact if that be the case.
I would hug him, lower my head then raise it and smile and say thank you.
Then I would buy him a cup of coffee and set back and chat if the chance will allow.
This is dedicated to my offspring herewith this book of poetry.
Just be happy that you got the chance to be.

TABLE OF CONTENTS

Chapter	Page
A Matter of Time	1 - 2
Attraction	3 - 4
Beginning	5 - 6
Cup	7 - 9
Dream	10 - 11
Elements	12
Friendship	13 - 14
For Real "Though"	15 - 16
For the Taken	17
Happy Mother's Day	18
I Need Not See	19 - 20
Keep Dreaming	21 - 22
Let Me Ride	23 - 24
Love and Care	25 - 26
More or Less, More or Less	27 - 28
Notice	29 - 30
On My Mind	31 - 32
Pass Your Way	33 - 34

Patience	…………………………………………	35
Something Anew	…………………………………………	36 - 37
Stand Down	…………………………………………	38 - 40
Taste	…………………………………………	41 - 42
The Bridge	…………………………………………	43 - 44
The Corner	…………………………………………	45 - 47
The Observer	…………………………………………	48 - 49
The Side of Another World	…………………………………………	50 - 51
Things	…………………………………………	52
Time	…………………………………………	53 - 54
Time is Ticking	…………………………………………	55
Thinking	…………………………………………	56
Acknowledgement	…………………………………………	57 – 59

THE STORM THAT GOT ME THINKING

Well, this is what I want to say, this is my short story. I got caught up by this storm in 2014 on or about January the 28th. Went to purchase two tickets at Center Stage, it was closed, so I went to the Civic Center, downtown in the ATL.

I knew it was slated to be a somewhat bad ice-covered day. The weather forecast was on point and warnings were all loud and clear. Cautioning all to hunker down and get off the roads. It was because this certain entertainer was on top of his game, man he was smoking every venue, with a sold-out performance at every stop. I had never been to one of his shows and I wanted to impress my friend with tickets to the event, who truly wanted to see him.

I think the tickets were for the Philips Arena performance. To tell the truth, I was trying to impress a true lady friend. She wanted to see the show and as a nice guy on most requests that I can muster, if I can, I will.

Call me a sucker if that is what I am, because most nice guys are. Sometimes I know it, then I think ninety-five percent (95%) of the time, I don't. So, I'm just a five- percent (5%) brainer.

No need to hate if I am the one who offered to help. For not one person has ever done enough injustice for me to Truly, Truly, Truly. Now I'm only talking about ME, "don't get it bent out of shape."

I would do poems all the time, but I do not know where it was then or is now coming from within me. Because I'm no poet, you feel me? He is, that other "Joe" guy on the other universe inside.

I think he has been here before and is now using me as a host, for a good spirit shall never vanish for it is part of the universe, it moves from time to infinite time.

As all spirits.

My daughter said I should "write down my poetry". My brother-in-law Allen said….. I was, well, you know, I hope my sister stop cooking for him too.

So, that is why I did not want to do those extra romantic poems, but I think next time I will, only if the inner spirit beckons my labor.

I owned an old flat bed six tire commercial truck; it was a good running baby too. No major mechanical problems other than no heat. But that was okay because I always dressed for the occasion. Here in the ATL I used it as my money maker hauling wooden pallets and cardboard boxes.

So, I did a short-day morning's work, just to get off in time to make the trip downtown to the ATL from Riverdale, Clayton County Georgia. This is the same location as that of Hartfield Jackson International, the best.

Now, I was thinking after looking at the sky, it was smooth and pleasant. Just a thirty (30) minute ride or an extra (15) minutes max. Get the tickets a jet back home in about one hour forty-five (145) minutes max round trip.

So, I went to Center Stage to purchased them, bad timing, I purchased them elsewhere. Then it was coming down like a winter storm.

"Lovely" I said to myself. I started home from downtown and by then traffic was crazy and my gas was low.

I filled my tank then hit the road again headed to Interstate 75 / 85 South. Good timing, but things were then bumper to bumper.

I decided to take the city streets, bad decision. So, after about two hours in city traffic going in a circle. I went somewhat Southwest on M-L-K towards Interstate 285, bad decision, but I was tripping and was out of it at that point.

Ice was all over the place, and I mean "all over the place." Things were very bad. I reached I-285 around 5:30 p.m. Yeah, "I'm so smart," what a nut case I was. On a slow day in the metro ATL it's busy, with ten hundreds of thousands of people on the road.

Man, this is the mecca for all walks, the black ice on that day just added to the slide. I took it in as something that will only happen a few hits to me, in this, my lifetime.

This is the ATL. Stop your go, that it did, tamper down the flow, that it truly was. This place extends out forever, over several metro counties. Clayton, Cherokee, Cobb, Dekalb, Douglas, Fayette, Forsyth, Fulton, Gwinnett, Henry, and Rosedale all trapped in one Atlanta, Georgia, just to name a few.

Traffic was bumper to bumper, ice all over the Interstate. I had no heat in my truck, it was bitter cold. I wore a coverall jumpsuit that protected me from the extreme cold weather. I wore two dollar gloves that keep my hands warm and had on two pair of wool socks in my work boots.

It was kept dark tight and cold, but lights were on the freeway, that was a blessing for all. There was this one lady driving a small SUV, she could not gain traction on the ice due to not so good tread on her back tires. She was also in the inside left lane trying to drive too fast and was spinning out. So, I asked her to allow me to help her. She drove then into the shoulder lane just in front of my truck as we headed South on the Interstate.

I pushed her vehicle with my truck for about four miles or more, it seemed like a hundred miles, but it was not. I slowly pushed her SUV for almost eight hours, inch by inch, foot by foot and yard by yard. I had to let her go, I didn't have any other option, my gas was now near the caution zone in my own tank.

Next, I helped this young guy with a jump start. I got on Interstate 285 around 5:30 p.m. from M-L-K got off unto Camp Creek Parkway at 3:15 a.m., almost some ten hours later. It was an event I will never forget.

There was no need to call for help because help could not get to that spot, unless by air, period. It was self and self only, but there were people from all walks of life who could help and did indeed help others in need. So many just got out of their vehicles and walked away, with no other options I figured, no choice.

The best part of this was being able to help others, including money for gas and food for some who were hungry with no money. I took a nap on the floor at the RaceTrac on Camp Creek Parkway just West of I-285. People were everywhere.

Not one person out of order, "not one." When daylight arrived, I put gas in my tank and gave a guy a ride home. His car was stuck in the medium, as there was no tow in sight, it was only about a few miles from our location. By then the sun was shining and things was getting back to normal, so to speak.

I then headed home, to Saratoga Pl, Riverdale GA, again.

But one thing I noticed, out of all of this, the ice, snow, traffic, the cold, the time spent in those long lines, again, not one person got out of order, not one, from all walks of life.

Thank you, RaceTrac, best decision I ever made.

A MATTER OF TIME

We are informed that an atom is a small mass of energy that can produce untold results. That first this hidden compound, so small but giving time to connect, it will bring forth visual wonders, when united with its destined building block, to be connected just in a matter of time.

We should understand that an atom too, got its origin from a mass as infinite in time passed. A dark hole, where gravity tames its capture as time matters not.

We begin our journey not knowing sometimes where it will end. Some short, carved from an ever-endless voyage. Yet it too will subside, as all things created from an atom in a matter of time. Matter encompasses a space of its own. Large and small or just maybe in-between.

The smallest equation of this in itself is an atom. At its center core, feathered out as far as time will expand. Equal on all axis, as a matter of time, from start to end.

When given a clock to set and plot a course to take that trip of life, be real with it, not only to one's - self. For an atom will always be here, yet the makeup will gradually change and over time indeed it too, surely shall vanish.

That is sure to happen in, *"A Matter of Time."*

ATTRACTION

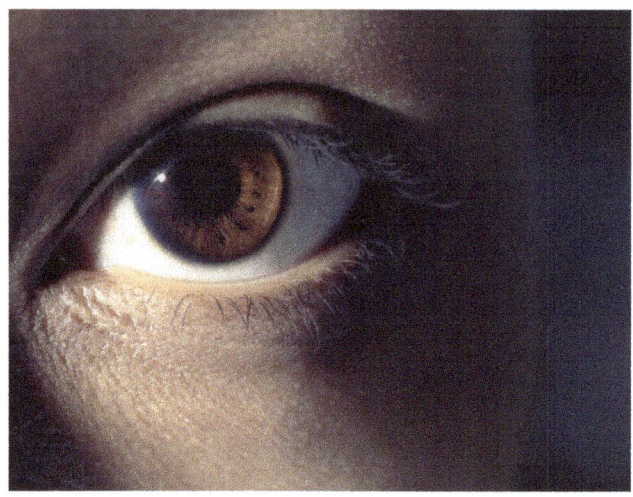

The world is filled with things that will attract us all. If we would just allow ourselves the time to set back and allow the mind to first explore.

As we gaze at the sky above some of us may sometimes wonder, what makes that shining ball of fire that emits so much intense heat? Why is it that a star so distant, yet so shiny and visual so many million stars away? That "star," referred to as a "moon" set so gracefully above.

Attracts all forms of attention from humans to the smallest creatures crawling, known to woman and mankind as well. The attraction is that of the beginning of creation, that magic is untold.

That attraction takes you back to the dreams of Ancient Being.

As we witness our now existence that spirit has never faded away. That moon glow is the hard rock foundation of who we are today.

She the moon, is the birthplace of all. He the sun, thereafter, provide the strength to make and develop that needed energy to grow. Both affixed in that heavenly body above at all sides, as well as beneath and below, put in motion many light years, eons ago.

Time has no measures to its start, as well, if and when it will automatically come to an end.

Between this spear and moments in creation a single star appears to fill a void in space. For this creation too, indeed was also meant to exist. As with all things of this vast universe were predetermined to be.

You.

BEGINNING

From the thoughts of togetherness, to gather for just a desire to bond. Not thinking, or if that be the case. Venture out, just to please that somewhat heated desire to unite.

Now as we both expect to achieve an end to that pending thirst and now warmed inner quests to just let go. We care not the outcome, for now it is only pure pleasure sought, for that is truly the start of it all.

The foundation is somewhat shaky, the footing is as slippery as being affixed on a steep rocky slope, filled with nothing but unfrozen butter, with hearts so heated to help that sure slippery fall.

While doing so, make sure to hold on tight. Reach out and be not worried.

Worry not, as gravity has for now taken hold, enjoy the ride. For the beginning is now passed.

Let go of just that, separate from the slide, catch hold to a firm rock.

Do not be depressed, for it just might bring about too much slide. Calm the waters, figure it out, then just downplay the game.

Just hold on tight, adjust if you might, for all happy beginnings, should always have a truly happy End.

CUP

Capture the essence of that flavor when the desire to taste overwhelms your inner fiber to just say, why not.

To think of what matters not when controlling is to farfetched to even sustain the drive needed to master all the inner power just flexing that deep hinged concept of, why not.

Stop, set back, and relax in a place of quiet peace, open up your soul then count to three.

Look straight ahead, then let out a sigh of constant relief. Inhale once more as you touch your inner spirit, for it is that your Inner - Being that brings you to exist and to be.

The makeup is that part which forms the surroundings to capture that expected filling.

No matter the size or origin. The purpose is the exact same. Dare not intrude, less be that of preparedness, for if so, that inner mixture just might erupt.

Do not dwell on the unpleasantries of life, be oh so thankful that you exist just to be a part of this vast universal plain. Fault not those who made it possible for your existence. For if not for their Prior - Being, would you also just happened to be?

Unlock all that is abundantly good, for it is there. Open up and just let it be. Uplift all, not tear down, for just a few second of understanding shall change the flow of that which seems bad, to good.

Up-end all sorrow, do not allow it to be that of the case for total displeasure. For happiness is the key to all. Pretend not to favor, then turn - a - back as we then proceed to tear down. Point in a direction of growth, lend a hand to pull along if you can.

The bottom is always constructed to capture its given prey, for it is indeed a willing host.

The cup is designed with all entrapments complete, sides and bottom only. An outlet atop to escape, for the surroundings are designed to maintain that captured intended and ready to fill from bottom to top.

When all that is abundantly full. Bottoms Up.

DREAM

As I just set back relax and think. I now have just suddenly slipped into a deep submissive sleep. I am somewhat aware of my surroundings, yet I rather stay in a semi unconscious state. With visions of what has now taken me into this relaxed zone.

I can now see things that only my vision can unfold, even with my eyes so firmly shut. My body so relaxed, now I concentrate only in one direction. As now, it is an effortless task.

For the toils of life has now long past. Just relaxing now, as I dream of none other than you. I can see reflections of so many lovely images of none other, than you. As I just whispered sweet nothing into your Ear.

Oiled your soft body with that gentle touch from the tip of your head to the bottom of your feet.

Smile, as I dare not awake not now, for if and when I do it's just a dream, and as I do know with the right chemistry some dreams do come true.

Move close my lady, don't stand off too far, so as to allow this smile now on my face, planted so deep in my mind, will be visual for you "AS Well."

ELEMENTS

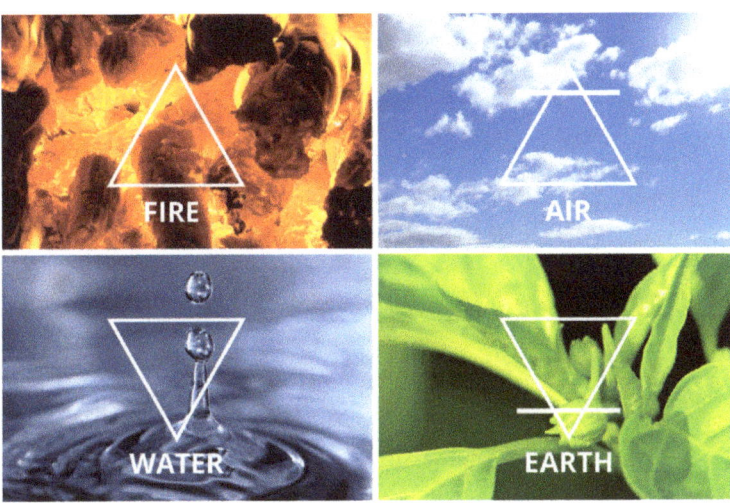

Surrounding all, is an air of both pleasure on one hand and one of open caution, on the other. Awaken to the feeling of gratitude, to just say "the lights are still bright." Be mindful of yesterday and the days yet to come. Prepare oneself internally, then set out to bend the curve.

The feeling of so much open space, yet the surroundings are oh so extreme, having been tilted to the axis of imbalance, for the master plan has moved a bit off center. Exit, then inhale deep, as one will hold a second longer than the one just a before moment connected to the same.

Stand tall and walk firm, clean away that which has collected dust and now holds not a reason to truly maintain or just enjoy. Open up the door, then enter the center of all. Turn around three times, then stop, go back just one turn, as the previous turn before. To reposition the inner and outer, will center life.

As the elements of all are the makeup of a simple part of Just - Being.

FRIENDSHIP

In a time of Friendship, the stars are positioned to shine upon it all.

In a time of Friendship, the moon is always Oh so bright, the clock exists not. The water flows as if the spigot will never turn off the flow. The wind blows with a smooth gentle cool breeze when the anticipation of each encounter touch one's face.

In a time of Friendship, one might just stand firm, might just back up, not even communicate, might just walk away. Then fall back on the real meaning, if that what it is truly about, "Friendship."

In a time of Friendship, the sun rise and never sets, the moon glow is bright, stars shines all day as well as night.

Reflection of smiles with each and every encounter, be it up close or distanced far apart.

When there is a need to vent, an ear open to hear, not any eyes closed. A mind to be more open, not a negative comparison to the past. To place a foot forward, not set back, feet crossed together, tilted, back hands crossed at back of neck, in a steep recline.

Not pointing a finger or placing one's ego on a stand perched just a foot above. Judge not, for words of encouragement is a much needed helping hand.

Look not for imperfections, for all have many. Cast not a net of steel, comprised with chains. Spread seed of sunflowers, for the expected bloom will always be that of pure delight, just to be associated with or a combination of.

In a time of "Friendship", I must not want or expect my style to cross over to that independent makeup of what brought this union first together. The time Friendship began as just that and if checked and maintained not wanting to be in control. "The Time Of Friendship Will Start And Never End."

FOR REAL "THOUGH"

I look at your picture and say to myself, with eyes closed and mind fold, as if time matters not. This day of work has come to an end. It's time to reflect before just another hard day begins. I make it to my place of peace, for I know when there, I can set back relax and soothe my mind and think of you.

As I allow the steam from a hot shower to take some body pain away. I enjoy the sound of a sweet mellow song, with glass in hand, red wine to enjoy, as I raise my treat high above my head and toast this very day.

My eyes yet closed, I now picture you standing there just inches away, with body and mind awaiting my smoothing gentle touch. As you smile, then softly and slowly brush your hair back with your fingers, as if with a brush, having every lock now in tack.

Then step in, your body so, soft so smooth, so flawless and so ready for my touch, awaiting that massage, as steaming water runs as it seems an everlasting flow, down your lovely, sculptured back.

With oil, hot in hand, I began to slowly drip it on those spots that beckons its slippery mix. I must not rush the moment, for if so, I just might spoil the pleasure we both now desire.

That sweet smell of you and your presence again summons up thoughts I have long placed so far back into my hidden thoughts of desire. It is now overflowing and time to withdraw.

Dare not hesitate, for now to delay will spoil the flow. I pause for a quick second or two, then gather my favorite "pastime" among so many that you have in store. Setback, just relax and inhale deep, then blow out slowly as the aroma of that smoke filled the Night Time Air.

FOR THE TAKEN

An apple is defined by taste, a good glass of wine is defined by constant age, a flower is defined by sight and smell, the day is defined by light as darkness relates to night. We see a star that glows in the distant sky, the moon glow that lights a path to travel. The rain to soothe the desire when it drowns a thirst. A storm to say it too has a place. The sun that warms and grows life. The world is filled with things to see and do. Not having enough time to plan, design, build, enjoy to see or touch all that this universe has to offer. Yet, if given the chance, why we are here, one should take time to pleasure ourselves. After all, that is what life gives, the chance for us to Do.

HAPPY MOTHER'S DAY

A mention of feeling is one that expresses CARE. A thought of kindness, tells the story of Inner - Being. A hand out-reached beckons a touch. With arms open wide, is a call to unite. When we love, that's a sign to be afforded to all mankind. The true meaning of this and much – much more care will be placed in a GOLD BOTTLE and placed with "care," in that universal ocean of love, not just to you or myself, "But For All."

I NEED NOT SEE

With eyes closed and arms fold, the wind blows forcefully not. Is it day or is it night? The clock with time now stands motionless. It puzzles me for now, as that cool breeze of summer rush across my face.

My sense has now altered me of what surrounds me, or just what it is, or who has now, entered my space.

I dare not open my eyes, nor open my mouth to question my thoughts. For I know this is not yet the time or place. Just move a bit closer my dear.

Breathe in, as I enjoy that scent of smell. I feel a body of motion, as it circles my mind, as if I were in space, suspended in time.

To reach out now would be in vain.

Not yet close enough to truly discover, or what promises to make, or how much time is would take, to have, protect and hold.

I will not question that sweet smell, no not yet, for time will tell if it will just fade away. As with a fresh flower, it is seasoned to bloom.

My mind can indeed taste your sweet nectar, as I gather a scent of your breathtaking everlasting natural perfume.

The thoughts of you now etched firmly in my mind. I need not touch my dear, for now I know that it is you. For I have touched you, I have held you close, I have been with you now, in so many pleasant ways, only I myself will ever know.

I have even had the pleasure, of your sweet taste.

No not physically my dear, yet just to have you near, the smell of your presence my lovely lady, is like hearing sweet angels, sing songs from Heaven - in - my "Ear."

KEEP DREAMING

Just as I look around my smell captures the essence of a flavor that slowly passes by. Your aroma is breathtaking, its one that makes me stand firm in my tracks as if I were in quicksand, stuck firm, not able to sink, as it holds me fast.

An angel extends a smile across her face of pure delight. Eyes that burn deep inside, with a reflection of silver as with the lining of a fresh summer shower. Steadfast that lovely flower, that perfume. Time now stands still as she walks, then as she passes and moves so gently by. So "QUIET" one need not figure her journey or path, for that everlasting fragrant will forever be.

Mind boggling and so captivating, I begin to search the voids deep within my thoughts, as to what this unfound treasure could be, if in fact it can truly be determined at all. Impressed with that style, that skin so GOLD and Clear.

Your hair so natural, as it is now styled back as to not cover up that unblemished non-made-up sculptured face.

Nothing can be as sweet as everlasting pleasure, from start to end, to just stand firm, I dare not confront or impede, for to do this will surely disrupt that flow.

The desire to touch or come too close just wanting to figure out, if it is that lost nectar of the universe. A collection of flavors, as I now gather my temptation, then compose my sanity.

As I am now awake, I have discovered who has just entered my inner thoughts and planted that seed and walked pass and etched my heart with that everlasting memory each time I close my eyes.

I can just lean - back and take it all in. I better not hurry for if so, I just might not experience your real flavor again.

End this dream now, I must, for it is time to "MOVE ON."

LET ME RIDE

As you begin this journey, you set out on an uncharted course of what you hope and expect the end shall be. You are somewhat unprepared to trek, yet it's time to expand the clock, as the second hand moves as swift as this Earth orbits this universe, for which it is captured to do.

Prepared not, for you are depending on an outward source among other beings to feed that desired to control, for its what's inside you and yourself only.

As you come to this wide road, first reluctant to cross. I pick you up and save you cost, for you see no reason to sweat.

The river you must cross, yet with no boat, not even a single oar. My back is now your support. For I tread so well, as I will take you across now with pleasure. I dare not falter, for you must reach that other shore. The mountains are mighty, with snow caps too cold to bare. "Can I take you there, all the way up and across to that valley on the other side?" You again ask of me, though not out loud, but way deep down inside.

"Wait, you can't?" As you now frown in displeasure and disbelief. That's okay, "I will move on and find another Jackass who surely can," as you state so very loud.

Your desire is well taken, my dear friend, I truly do, UNDERSTAND.

LOVE AND CARE

A mention of feeling, is one that expresses care. Thoughts of kindness, tells the story of inner being. A hand out reached beckons a touch. With arms open wide, that is a call to unite. Do not hesitate stepping forward, when the feeling is meant to be shared and the mention of love is expressed out loud, for all to hear.

For the word love is connected with kindness. The gift of love is to understand those not connect to one's, daily ritual of that inner desire to touch and bond. To forget those unpleasant moments, then move on to a better understanding in search of what is the true meaning of care.

Be not one who looks to obtain passion, then reject the request to do the same.

Allow not the makeup or the birthplace of a stranger determine your inner soul. For we should look not to control.

Love is to look all in the eye to say, if but only to yourself "I am of the same blood, just a different line." For we all should understand and know the true difference from the word "love" as to being "in love." For that position my dear friend can sometimes make a worldly difference.

When we love, that's a sign to be afforded to all. No matter what, no matter the reason, no matter the cause, no matter the ups or downs, no matter the ins or outs.

Sometimes things get crossed up in the battle for a perfect outcome. We must seek to unite, if that is indeed the purpose at hand. United, we all should stress, from start to end.

For if we love and care for ourselves, then we should also have the same for others, even if not, though hard to do.

The true meaning of this and much -much more love, will be slowly placed in a gold bottle with "Care," into that universal ocean of "Love."

Not just for you or myself, but for all "Woman And Mankind."

MORE OR LESS, MORE OR LESS

When I look at what life is, it's about what one can do to stand the test of time. When I close my mind, it's about opening up my heart to see what surrounds me. When I tell a story, it's about finding out what is ahead. When I speak sometimes, it's about relaxing the soul. When I stress so hard, it's about what is not needed to make my day. When I walk the path, it's about the plan that is made not to alter. When I talk too much, it's about the fact of yarn.

When I spend too much, it's about time to stop. When I stop to cry, it's about time past and the memories of displeasure and joy. When I tell a lie, it's about a fact of ploy. When I hold it back, it's time to let go. When I give a hand, it's a sign of care. When I smile, it's about the child inside. When I tell my plan, it's about what I wish the future would hold and unfold.

When I say what I will do, I must try, yet hurt no one, then if I do hurt, my time here is made up of a fake and a fraud.

When I step out, I must prepare to make a stand. When I fall back, then is the time to say go pass. When I reach out, I tend to seek. If I gather the mass, then it's time to share.

The sun shines, the moon glows, the rain falls, the wind blows, the lake forms, and the river flows. The ocean is wide, more yet the sea is deep. When night falls, then, the stars shine, clouds forms, the thunder roars, lightning strikes, the earth shakes, when the quake awakes, the mountain trembles, when its inner core erupts.

All seasons will change, as all created matter will do. Time is vast, as with an endless black hole, life is short.

Too much to see, too much to do, too much to have, too much to hold, too much to fight and far too much to enjoy.

But this is the plan for I did not create me, I am just another element formed from the seeds of Woman and Man.

Look way deep inside, don't hide, we all have a purpose, so put it to task, turn my back not, because, if I do, very soon my time here will go past.

"I must try and that I will."

NOTICE

As I look out a window of hope my eyes catch a vision of you. When I think of one's life's treasures all filled with solid gold. Your lovely smile, etched deep as with the Earth's core.

When it rains things sometimes do come apart. When a strong wind blows, it can cause a flower to glide. The movement of a foundation will sometimes cause a structure to shift.

Movement to the left or right, will sometimes alter the center.

But for you my sweet thing, I will always come back to that same place, that same space so tight and so sound, that same foundation. That exact spot that got it started in the first place. "You".

ON MY MIND

As if the Moon's light will never subside, to touch its glow will melt my heart away. Akin to a fallen virgin snow flake, on a cold, but sunny winter's day.

Affectionate is what you are, it keeps me wondering if indeed that too, will ever vanish, be removed, or just fade away. Understanding your inner soul, as if your mass were one of solid gold, to shine forever and ever. To touch your flame, that inspiration you give forth just when I am oh so near.

Reminiscent of the joy of the past, as with the present, you make my smile so everlasting, even if I'm not awake, being fast asleep, behind a pleasant dream. I care not to move too soon, for I know the future will hold nothing but that of pleasure.

I yarn for the next time you are near. To touch, to see, or just capture that flavor of your sweet mixture, with your universal charm.

Appealing, is what you are, as with a fresh rose, from a soft seasoned rainfall; as a rainbow appears, in the distant sky. Like a white dove in flight, with wings spread wide.

An Angel, is just who "You Are,"

PASS YOUR WAY

It all started from a thought. The beginning is that exact point in time we paint what existence that is surely bestowed upon us all.

Swift as a falling star, then vanished in the milky-way. Its origin shall be not determined, not yet. For in the flicker of an eye, life now captured that final orbit, if indeed that is what it just might be.

As we began this journey of life, we know not what it will entail. We chart a course only if we have been given the ability to do so. With the anticipation of the finer things, for which we all pray and seek this precious life will bring forth.

Yesterday's thoughts, to sustain all that this universe has opened up to offer.

As much as all preconceived thoughts of mankind was destined to hold and at the end of a long journey unfold. Long, long, long, and so very long ago.

At the start was the bottom of all. Planted in darkness awaiting to be propelled far away from the beginning of time. A very special place, this one point is that of which can never be conceived. Not from its origin, nor in-between.

This trek shall be as stars gathered around a shining moon, filled with everlasting light. Time will indeed change things for all.

We must realize, there will be a time of sorrow, for us all. That is truly a part of the same. We must truly enjoy this journey, take advantage of what is at hand. Do not despair, for when we go pass.

For we will and shall be together forever and forever more. Leave memories of love for others to follow. As some dreams do in fact come true.

Love all, and life will be as it just got started, and the spirit of life that will never, never end.

Smile in pleasure, for we all must gather our treasures of life, then put aside for a "Better Day."

PATIENCE

A patch in a long road, is what it's all about. A tiny pebble in a hard rock of love. Just a dark cloud and such a never ending sunny day. When the rain starts to fall, it's just a few drops of pleasure, to wash the dust away.

On a very cold day, warmth shall be injected just in the nick of time, so as not to freeze that heart so rich with care, it too will beat even faster and pound like a drum as you hold your chest and smile, then close your eyes, for summer is around the corner, as you spring to your feet, better not fall, for that my lady, is a few more months away.

As the seasons change, so will a flower in a pot of soil. But one thing you can be sure of my dear. "Good Things Comes To Those Who Wait."

SOMETHING ANEW

You ever hear the phone ringing and then think to yourself, I'm just dreaming, because you had just fallen asleep only a few seconds before?

Have you ever been walking and stop dead in your tracks, gasped your mouth opened wide and eyes affixed in a gaping dead straight stare unable to even blink, but whispered out loud, "I know I have been here before?"

Do you ever sometimes think way deep down inside your fiber of those caved up thoughts, it is time I venture out farther than I have been so protected to do the same before?

Well, the past is just that, the past, time for me to pass it by. "I know for sure what I can bring forth, as I welcome this wonderful new point in time."

As I kick the dust off of those old, cemented ways, "I will just start anew each day and thereafter as the days before." Be very happy to have made it to this day, to simply say to all mankind.

Enjoy the time here on this planet Earth, for its a wonderful place to be. Take care of all that is important, for it too can vanish in the blink of an eye. Life is a gift to us all, do not take it for granted, as told "we only have one."

Make not a resolution to place yourself in a trench. Just be real with self and all will come your way. Remember to just lend a hand when you can. Don't be so outspoken and judge not that which we truly do not know the score or understand.

Ask not the purpose of a gift to others, just reach in your pocket, and give something of value with no questions asked, if you can.

For those without, may just one day be back on their feet, away from the ground for now, where they call home, plus a place to sleep.

Let us always remember, "give from the heart, "a Medium of Exchange," and we "will receive."

Let's help the homeless, some of us have been there as well.

"Have A Blessed And Happy New Year, Here Now And Hereafter To Come."

STAND DOWN

As if we wonder how this universe got its origin, we too, can imagine the same for that of a child.

A child is the result of a complex mixture of genetics. That DNA is just a carbon copy of those who's intermixture of genes formed what is now created. Those chromosomes are like those unique threads united to create a woven blanket.

Nature began as a virgin, with no imperfections whatsoever. Yet the influx of human beings in conjunction with this universal gift, has BEFORE, NOW, and FOREVER tainted the creator's creation, that flawless gift given to man.

As in the past, as now and in the future to come. It is man and man alone, who will destroy this gift. Nature will never bring about its demise, never. Only humans selfish desire to tame the

elements above and below, shall as in the past, present and days to come, will surely repeat said man's again self-imposed demise.

Nature has its internal unique filters to dispose of any and all unwanted invaders, as truth-be-told. As we all have knowledge of the fact that" WATER IS A FORM OF NATURE."

Now again, as before, in ones' lifetime Human - Being is now at an apex of helplessness. Just setting back, "thinking" of what's next across the horizon, to contemplate that next move at this juncture seems like a crossroad searching for that true direction one must take.

A PUZZLING decision to step into tomorrow with open eyes and a cautious mind bent on what this now infected world has now surely bound all mankind.

Man creates nothing, there is "nothing new beneath the sun." Only a given ability for a few and a very few, will be allotted to seek and discover what hidden treasures secretly set aside for man's existence and survival. But take advantage and misuse of such will surely be withdrawn in time.

Association is sometimes a matter of choice, if not controlled by another. If given the freedom to just step away at the appropriate time if that connection be one of demise, then step away. Do not allow a negative input be that of your master plan.

Testing the waters should determine the depth before we step off into something that just might be too deep. Too ruff to tread, too mighty to swim, from start to end. For our history is a sure sign of what might come to bare again.

A clear indication of the past as well as now being, will also project what the future could be as well. From its start, sometimes the bottom is where some things will begin.

Separate from that which will hinder the drive in a direction of prosperity. For that alone, could falter a direction meant to be uplifting.

Adaptation is a mental thing; it requires the mindset to dig in. For it is man and man alone who has now dealt a deadly blow to not only himself, but to "Generations Here And Hereafter To Come."

TASTE

You walk in, dressed in all black. That reflection of all that is pure, as thoughts of pleasure now just entered my desire to taste. Not knowing the origin from where you began your journey.

You now have captured my attention so I say softly to my inner-self, "better step forward now, for if not, when and if you turn and walk quietly out that door, this may never again come my way."

Step forward, I must, with head held high. No fear of rejection, for if so, I could say, if to no one but just myself, "it was better to have stepped forward, than not." "It was better to venture out, than not, at all." "It is better to have said very quietly to myself, why not," for if I do and succeed, my desire to test the waters might have just been placed on a temporary hold.

Failure, I think not. If so, I then would just pick up the broken pieces of this now crumbled heart, due to my non-intended stumble. At least it is better to have tried and failed, than not to seek a taste at all.

That black crown of pearls atop your sculpture, is pure delight. No mixture of outside, being all natural as you tilt from side to side. All thoughts of pleasure, for it is just what the gods envisioned, from that true concept of Your - Being.

That smile too, seems so pure as well, no faults, no errors, no missteps, and no regrets.

Your graceful curves, steadfastly cement "Your - Being." For it is what your creation was truly meant to be. An encounter of a true Queen, for you were destined as such.

Your sweetness was created from a mixture of flavor, be alarmed not. From conception to reality, it is here to stay even when the clock stops.

Dare not sample a prolonged taste, for if so, I might capture that quest for just that, just that, just that and that alone.

Your sweetness shall never fade away no matter the influx of which is not suited to invade. It will forever be as that flavor of sweet honey affixed deep within your fiber.

Just that sweetness, if no other, even if "I Never Taste."

THE BRIDGE

I wake up, then look around, just to see if I'm indeed still alive. Sometimes I admit I take for granted, more often than not.

I get up, then erect my frame, as if it too, knows the score. Blink my eyes and wipe the sleep away from my crusty face.

As all sorts of things began to sink deep into this vast mind-bank of which I am so lucky to possess.

Ready myself, to exit my shelter of comfort, that I am so lucky to maintain. Time to venture out, for another day beckons my labor, whatever it just might be. One of leisure, or that of toil, one that is somewhat planned and most that is often not.

I think all shall be well as like that yesterday and the days before. Listen now as I do in order to understand what I observe.

As I travel on this road, one of which I have been accustomed of doing so - so many times, both days and nights then back to my shelter of tranquility, one of happiness and peace. I notice things to my left and right, sometimes more often than not. I sometimes peak

into my rear-view mirror, to make sure the distance behind me is that of the past. Sometimes a sign of yellow prep me to now expect a red reflection to caution a stop. As I stand steadfast green signals my now continued flow.

In the back of my mind, as I enjoy the sound of music on my radio. I sing along, for happy-go-lucky, that is who and what I am. I think of what I shall do on this day, as I have so many times before.

Just to make this day go past, then back to my palace at the end of a long hard day if that is the case.

It is so early in the day. I can still recall several pleasant dreams for the night before.

Enjoy whatever I have and whatever I do. Just make sure I do not step on another person's feet, in doing so. In short, I shall never know my day, when the bridge of life shall fall. "Enjoy Life."

"Never Forget Miami."

THE CORNER

It's a well-known mathematical fact that the end to a solution if in search of true happiness is well stated "the shortest distance between two points is a straight line. "As one plus one makes the even number "two." We are well informed, if rain falls, there must be moisture within the clouds above, when darkness falls, one requires light to see the way.

It's a well-known fact, the "seasons will bring about change," yet the inner mixture of the elements above and below will alter nature's time as well. When something is hot, at times it just might turn cold. As a shadow fades into the dark, as with a sweet apple fallen from a tree.

When time itself seems to stop; as a seed planted beneath the soil, awaiting nature to push the clock. Speed will generate heat when its path is long, if given the energy to propel the drive.

It too shall end, as with new life and all thing that has the chance to begin over time. Growth is a sure thing, rather good or bad, if given the time to develop into whatever given purpose unfold.

It is a well-known fact, the sea is deep, that rivers are born to flow, that a flower when given water will help it grow. That birds have wings and love to fly, that fire will heat the space when contained and sometimes burn. Water will put it out, yet if left to simmer and linger around too long, that same blaze just might return.

The larger the space the more it takes to fill, yet small things can sometimes bring worldwide joy as with a new discovery just to see a small child smile, when given a simple toy.

Gravity has its way of sustaining its hold, motion allows things to go, time will bring about change. The stars shines both day and night, the moon glows to give us light, the sun give heat, as well the earth sometimes trembles beneath our feet.

On a cool day, a summer breeze appears, then set back, when clouds forms, the rain might fall yet, sometimes after the thunder roars and lighting flash, that's just a fragmented part of nature's flow.

It's a well-known theory, the universe is endless, and all things must come and all shall someday pass. That the present is now, tomorrow we know not what it shall hold. We quest to figure it out, what makes this system go, as we seek to charter a new tomorrow built on yesterday's dreams.

Like a newly discovered Black - Hole, turning in space for an infinity on a long straight road with no end in sight.

Now I venture into a new direction. I have started a new chapter, as I tell myself don't go back, for my past is just that, the past. Move forward I must journey a new road. Build on a new beginning, for the light ahead seems oh so very bright.

The circles are no more. The curves are now straight. For I have discovered true point to point that life has to offer.

This is really how life should be, I have turned the corner.

Why Not Come Join Me?

THE OBSERVER

For those of us who observe and to our mind say, "wish that it was me instead of him." For those of us who observe and to our mind say, "I know the solution," yet not understanding the problems.

For those of us who observe and to our mind say, "she will never make it, there is just no way." Why do we observe with smile on face, yet we are bitter at heart? With our arms open wide, but our soul so cold. With an ear to hear, then quickly turn away, not walk softly but run then hide?

Why do we offer solutions to the task at hand, for if we would step forth, would we too, do the same? Why do we smile at face and very soon thereafter frown in displeasure? We speak of encouragement, yet we think to discourage all the same.

We watch you build, for in time we will have joy to see you fall down. We hear your plan, then question only ourselves on how you can truly make it work?

For we all must be aware that the test of life is not meant to just throw away. It is a thing we all must grasp and treat it as a mountain of nothing but pure treasure. Is it because our labor is forty, yet theirs times ten?

Is it because we wish them to fail, just to make their story of success a lie? When we ourselves, just set back and then observe, but have not the courage to give it a try.

For those of us, when deep down into our fiber just do that, observe, because that is truly what and who we are "Observers." Then say to ourselves as well to others. "I am an observer, who can only "observe" thereafter judge."

Do not judge me, because I do not set back, and observe, then thereafter, judge others. For I truly know not their life's task at hand. For I have not traveled their path, nor taken up their mantle.

For my quest is my quest alone.

For I know "THE TRUE OBSERVER," do you?

THE SIDE OF ANOTHER WORLD

Do you ever wonder what it would be like if our world as we now know it would be as a drop of rain vanished in the dark abliss with forever memories etched with thoughts of pleasure for what we have enjoyed in this distant world long past?

Would that world not yet found or not yet having a place for one to connect with all its surroundings as now the world we know. Could this world be suited for one's pleasure created out of grace from the almighty to whom we search above?

Having not yet time to travel, to explore, to venture out, to search and find what is now this place we call Earth. To compose all that this present world has to offer. To some if given time, when asked the question.

Does it offer anything at all?

Indeed, it does.

Do you ever wonder or imagine falling out of time as in space turning and turning to realize that when mass falls the drop is headed for the Earth's foundation suited to capture the fall?

This world formed so many light years past, so many suns, stars, planets so many moons, if that was the case at hand. Created to enjoy, to explore, to breathe in. It is here forever and ever, as with one very tiny drop of paint on a huge, eclipsed wall, blended in as evening sets and all present shadows falls.

Capture, then enjoy the flavor allotted by this world, it is what arms open wide, beckoning those who can and wish to heed the offer of pleasure. Dare not turn - a - back then step away, for if so when turned around the chance for everlasting joy, might not come this way again.

Be strong if you can, chart and plan the specs at hand, just know what to do. Look up high, for the world's roadmap is seated in the heaven above. There are two sides to all.

"When One Stops To Visit This World, You Will One Day Venture To That World On The Other Side."

THINGS

When a seed is planet, it takes time to adjust, for its now host has surrounded all it may have to offer.

When darkness falls, we venture into a place of quiet, to allow our sight, to adjust to what has now captured the daylight just moments eclipsed.

A bird sings to give pleasure for it can only do so when all is well. Memory come in many forms, some of displeasure and others of nothing but pure delight.

Swift as a falling star, vanished in the milky way, its destination not determined. In the flicker of an eye, it is captured in that final orbit, if indeed that is what it just might be that of yesterday's thoughts.

Close your eyes my dear and dream of things to come. Then smile and count to three, open wide, reach out and soon and very soon, someone will be there just to take you there, to that place of NO RETURN.

TIME

As if the world we know will allow us time to explore, when given the tools of knowledge to ascertain its vast concept of hidden treasures.

To seek then explore the uncharted back darkness of not only one's inner thoughts, if allotted the chance to let go. Then venture out, one must indeed take heed.

Being not bound by ropes or restraints or confined by the capture of this Planet Earth's gravitational pull. For which we all are destined to be. Step out, for time seems short, yet the journey is oh so long.

As with space surrounding us all. Vision is two-fold, that in which with our eyes focus we shall see, as with them shut, then fall asleep one sometimes shall dream.

When deep sleep itself will provide a vision of things past, present, and then into the future we may someday also venture out.

Look around, pay close attention to the things you have at hand. Take heed of it all, for you are in control. Plant your seeds of vision in your inner soul, then allow its growth to explore the outer realms of your entire universe.

Be not "bound", enslaved, or oppressed.

Be not confined to your surroundings. Time to let go, for if not, it too will surely, "Pass You By."

TIME IS TICKING

Born to be part of an everlasting endless journey of one's existence on this universal infinite plane.

A new discovery of just that past being is a daily quest. The unfolding of that magical creation brings forth new light as if darkness has propelled that hidden treasure.

For now, it holds so much more for all to explore. As one contemplates what the heart, body, and soul, will and shall explore that vast Black – Hole, created to capture and forevermore hold all past Beings, as it shall and will do now and in the future, be assured in time it will do the same.

Need not worry, for man shall go into that orbit of unknown venture, shall enter that silent passage of joy, in due time. For when the manual clock shall tick not.

"Time Will Forever Pass."

THINKING

Today, as one imagine what tomorrow will hold, One just will never at this instance know. The charm of being is everlasting like that of a black hole, suspended in time forevermore.

When one set back then wonders if what surrounds us, is indeed what will also be affixed in existence of tomorrow, or will it be forever vanished like the blink of an eye. As with the beat of a heart given ones' average lifetime, three billion.

It's a millisecond of time that is assured to come and thereafter shall past from conception to end. Thinking thoughts are many, yet action has to cement its purpose. For "action speaks louder than words". Words take many paths if spoken as related to the true subject matter in so many universal forms.

As with a lovely flower at first sight, it will bring about so many thoughts as with all things that captures a moment for one to contemplate and thereafter connect.

To think is what One' does, just before taking that "Next Step."

Acknowledgement

Erek Kendall

Pallet Depot, Inc.

Otis Kendall
Pallet Depot, Inc.

otis.palletdepot@gmail.com has been in business for over 20 years located in the ATL, Georgia.

Without their trust in me, this book would not have been started, their gift of seed money, with no questions asked changed my world.

Thank you so very much, may you prosper beyond your wildest dreams.

Juan Cruz
JC PALLETS, INC.

Mr. Juan Cruz is the owner operator of JC Pallets, Inc. ATL, GA. Seven (7) years and counting.

Without their trust in me, this book would not have been started, their gift of seed money, with no questions asked changed my world.

Thank you so very much, may you prosper beyond your wildest dreams.

The Poet

Joseph Jones, born in Ensley, a neighborhood located in Birmingham, Alabama in 1954.

I can remember as a very small child some of those things most poor people can truly reflect back on. That was the start of it all.

The housing projects, kindergarten and thereafter attending first grade at then Council Elementary School in Ensley. As a child walking to and from school was a norm.

I will never forget rapping "the Maypole" on May Day. We skipped danced around this tall pole affixed in the ground while rapping ribbon to complete its destinated look.

As well as attending First Baptist Church of Ensley. This was the same church of the beloved pastor, the Rev. A. D. King, the brother of the beloved "Rev Dr. Martin Luther King Jr."

At the very young age of six (6), I received my baptism at the same church, right at the pulpit, it was filled with cold water.

As a child, attending church was a must. It was not a sometimes thing, but a strict will do, no matter what.

This was the same church where Rev. King was discovered unresponsive in his church's home swimming pool, First Street Baptist Church, there in Ensley, Birmingham, Alabama. A very young man, who left us way to soon.

As a very small child, I remember riding the transit bus system in Ensley with my grandparent. It was a requirement after boarding the bus to proceed to the back seating area as far as possible.

Sometimes if required for others to have seating we would stand. My treat when we traveled on the city bus was "Kellogg's Apple Jacks."

As a child, with my grandfather the beloved Rev. George Washington Jones, myself and my three brothers Harold, Gary, and Malcolm he was our namesake.

He was married to our mother's, Mrs. Matilda Shanklin Fields' mother, the foundation of my life, Mrs. Carrie Bell Peterson, Coleman ,Jones, my beloved grandmother.

Our grandmother's sister Mrs. Lutishia Shanklin, Neal, Perkins those three women, helped mold me and my brothers.

When I got out of character, they would quickly, with hands on, get me back - in - line.

Our mother, the wife of Mr. Tommie Lee Fields, my proud stepfather, the father of my two lovely and very smart sisters Tonie L. Jones Phillips and our younger sister Sherry L. Jones Stribling.

I never knew my birth father and I hold no regrets or harsh feelings.

I never missed a step growing up as a child or man.

One day playing in Ensley, Alabama. The next thing I realized, my brothers and I, along with our grandparents, were in this small-town Crawford, it was Mississippi, the same postal code of our church, Pleasant Grove Missionary Baptist Church.

At the age of seven (7); I began second grade at B. L. Moor High, those "EAGLES," located in the country. Nothing but woods and dirt roads, but I loved it all.

As an average student, a 3.0 grade point upon finishing high school at B.L. Moor. Located then in Oktibbeha County, Mississippi. I participated in the school's band, thereafter sports, track and field and played football for those "Eagles."

A Cub-Scout, I grew up as a member of The Boy Scouts of America, "on my honor I will do my best..."

We did a lot of walking both days and nights, the moonlight, and stars were our guiding light at night.

We did a lot of walking during daylight as well in those woods on those dirt roads.

Trekking miles and miles as a child, as well as everything required of us by our parents. You name it, we did it in those backwoods as children.

From cotton farming, corn farming, Polk wood hauling by the truck loads, hay grass hauling and bailing, hand milking cows, slopping hogs, feeding chickens, the garden, house cleaning and much, much more.

A Bachelor of Science Degree from Alcorn State University. Those purple and gold. "BRAVES" and the "SWAC", Lorman, Mississippi on May 15, 1977.

During my college days, my GPA allowed me as a student to experience working as a co-op at Grand Gulf Nuclear Power Plant, during its initial construction stage. Upon finishing college, I obtained my first true after college job working as a civil engineering drafts-man.

Thereafter, I gained employment with the United States Forest Service as a civil engineering field technician overseeing the development and construction of forest land roads and bridges construction, among other duties.

My wife, Mary P. Jackson Jones and I later moved to Houston, Texas. Working as a civil drafts-person until being caught up in a then economic downturn and being laid off.

I became independent thereafter. I knew I had to do me and just me to be independent. I did work for others, but it was just to get positioned to be my own point man. My first startup was "Majestic Janitorial Service", located in Houston, Texas and Metairie, Louisiana,

Then thereafter Jackson, Mississippi, the use car business as a small owner. Thereafter, it was the ownership of an Italian restaurant business, in Starkville and Jackson, Mississippi "Marvello's" a partnership with my high school best friend, Marvin Seals.

I learned the mortgage business, and became a licensed mortgage broker, "Peak Mortgage Company", Jackson, Mississippi.

Having always been the independent type. I got that from my grandmother, and I can't change. I have tried but it just want work, I can't stop being that way, independent. Too much for me to explain who I am and what I'm about.

In short, I am no better than the next person, just a bit different.

Poetry is my way of expressing my Inner – Being. It's that other person inside who has been here before but in another form.

That being, it's just about peace and happiness for then, now and in times to come.

Hope you enjoy this, my "THINKING," "A BOOK OF POETRY," BY JOSEPH JONES.

www.ingramcontent.com/pod-product-compliance
Lightning Source LLC
LaVergne TN
LVHW051040070526
838201LV00066B/4870